Slow Practice Will Get You There Faster

by
Ernest Dras

CIP - Kataložni zapis o publikaciji
Narodna in univerzitetna knjižnica, Ljubljana

796.342

DRAS, Ernest
  Slow practice will get you there faster : [link between
Ben Hogan's mirror practice and his slow motion drill] /
by Ernest Dras. - Maribor: TheSolarSweetspot, 2009

ISBN 978-961-269-072-4

245929472

© Ernest Dras 2009
Revised edition, 2018

Front jacked photograph used by permission of T.M. O'Connell

www.thesolarsweetspot.com

Table of Contents

Introduction

In the sacred Vedic texts of India, it is said that we are spiritual particles seated on a machine made of material energy. According to this, we are spirit souls residing in a body that is actually a machine. Our mind can be compared to a computer or an electronic instrument that is connected to a physical machine. In this book, we shall explore the process of how to most effectively train or program this machine (the physical body) as well as the electronic unit (the mind) in order to perform a complicated and precise physical task, the golf swing.

From the very outset, I want to make this important statement: The ideas presented herein, the methods and processes explained and detailed in this book, are not my inventions. These principles are universal and have been in existence for centuries. This is chiefly what makes them valuable, because, if they belonged only to me, they would almost certainly be flawed; new theories and invented principles rarely survive the test of time. My specific contribution is that I have discovered these principles, turned them into methods, and have applied them to a specific activity in an innovative and effective way. Primarily, this book is about the best method for learning to perfect the golf swing.

Here's how these realizations developed. I became involved in tennis when I was eight years old. The memories of those beginning years are positive. We had an enthusiastic trainer, and he was of good character. It took quite a lot to learn the strokes and motions without a ball, but that was his method.

Later we played tennis on a small court, sometimes with foam balls. We played other sports for the development of general coordination, and there were specific exercises with the ball and racquet for hand-to-eye coordination. If I were to now begin teaching young players, I would not teach them much differently than how I was instructed. After this beginning period of about three years, a more difficult time ensued.

In later years, I became a tournament player and, in this way, I was drawn deeper into the competitive spirit. There were winning moments of joy along with moments of anguish when I lost. The desire to become a successful competitor had become stronger and stronger, but somehow, like so many others, I hit the proverbial wall. We practiced a lot—sometimes twice a day when there was no school—but there was little improvement to show for it. I hardly remember any time when I was satisfied with my play. There was always something with my backhand spin, or serve that was not as precise and consistent as it should be; I used to volley only when absolutely necessary.

I had some good results in those years—I was a member of Yugoslavian junior team and junior champion of Slovenia—however, I did not consider myself to be a really good player. I had these results because the technique of other competitors was even worse than mine, and they were generally less patient. I was not making genuine advancement. From the beginning, I was practicing tennis at the local club; it had a long tradition, and there was something progressive about it.

Yugoslavia had some quality tennis players in its history, a few of them even on the highest level. Sometimes, I wondered how it was possible that we were not being taught basic principles about how to hit the ball. If there were some men who were aware of this knowledge (and the essential importance of it), they were unwilling to reveal themselves; that remains a mystery to me.

At that time, we were still living under Communist rule in Yugoslavia, and the management of sports clubs was very different from what it is today. There were many people doing everything voluntarily at that time, and the club covered expenses for trainers and our travels to tournaments. I am thankful to all my well-wishers and trainers who tried their best on my behalf during my early tennis career.

Unfortunately, some important knowledge was missing, and competitors such as myself suffered. I remember this being mentioned two or three times, but never in a way that crystallized its import. I was young, amenable, and unable to realize how essential that missing piece really was. Neither did the trainers know of it; they must have considered it a kind of myth with no pragmatic value. They would simply stress basics, considering the so-called missing piece to be part of the realm of imagination. However, that piece is real, and it is pure physics. If they would have realized its importance, I am sure they would never have allowed us to practice and play as we did; they would have forced us to learn and practice the correct way. In other words, "Advanced techniques are the basics mastered." (From the 17th century Samurai Code)

It was all like a curse; this knowledge now seems so self-evident to me. Back in the day, however, we could not realize it. This existential fact brought us so many hours, days, months, and years of frustration. When there is desire, and when it is not fulfilled, anger arises. There was so much foul language, destruction of costly racquets (sometimes throwing them twenty meters away over the fence onto the nearby street). It was crazy; we saw no way out of this darkness.

Awakening

At the age of about fifteen, my former trainer introduced me one book, <u>The Inner Game of Tennis</u>, written by Timothy Gallwey. It was the German version, and this former trainer's wife (she was teaching the German language) kindly helped me with its translation. It was my first glimpse into the mental aspect of the game, and about the human being in general. I found the book very interesting, and I tried some of its recommendations. Ultimately, however, I cannot say that it caused any big changes in my game. However, as far as I remember, this was the first book that forced me to think. Before that, I was not interested in books; it was just the matter of reading duty while going to school and nothing more.

When I neared my twenties, there were big changes in my life. I had to interrupt my tennis career, entering the army for one year. I did not practice as I had before during this military stint, and I had more time for thinking. I was a young, impressionable man with many questions about life in general. However, my prominent desire was still to better understand sports. In my tennis years, I was practicing as much as many stars in their youth, but I had to ask myself: Why was there such a disparity in quality of play? What were the tennis stars doing differently?

While serving in the army, I made friendship with a fellow who was also a sportsman; he was experiencing similar thing. He served in my unit, and he introduced me to a well-known book with the title <u>Siddhartha</u>, written by the German author Herman Hesse. I was impressed. In due course of time, I read the majority of his other books (<u>Steppenwolf</u>, <u>Demian</u>, etc.). Hesse was Eastern-oriented, so I became favorable to that way of thought. After finishing my service in the army, I came into contact with the underlying source of his Eastern thought and wisdom, Vedic literature. The most well-known example of this vast knowledge, especially in the West, is <u>Bhagavad-gita</u>. Not so long ago, I was surprised to find out a connection between <u>Bhagavad-gita</u> and the famous golf book (and movie based on it), <u>The Legend of Bagger Vance</u>.

In both the book and the movie, parallels are drawn between the battlefield of Kuruksetra, the place where the famous talk between Lord Krishna and Sri Arjuna took place, and the golf course. There is a caddy (Bagger Vance) who is supposed to represent Krishna, and there is a golfer (Junuh) who is supposed to represent the warrior Arjuna.

The book is far more recognizable in its relation to the <u>Gita</u>. For example, there is this excerpt from chapter 13, which was not in the movie: "'Put the clubs away,' Junuh said, in a voice nearly inaudible. 'I see no profit in them or this whole fool enterprise.' 'Your mind is clearly in torment, Junuh,' Bagger Vance spoke slowly and evenly. 'Tell me please: What is the nature of your complaint?' Junuh glanced up sharply at this word, which seemed to trivialize his emotion. 'It couldn't be more obvious, could it? This whole endeavor is a freak show. A joke. What good will any of it do me, or anyone attached to it?' Junuh's hands were trembling. He ran them in pain through his hair, eyes gazing hollowly before him into the dunes. 'What is ever gained by defeating, others? What can be gained here today? If I win, I take no pleasure, and if I lose . . .'"

This correlates to the first chapter of the Gita, which begins, "Arjuna said: 'O infallible Krishna, please draw my chariot between the two armies. I want to see who is present here, who is desirous of fighting, and with whom I must contend in this great battle.'" And later, "Arjuna said: 'My dear Krishna, seeing my friends and relatives present before me in such a fighting mood, I feel the limbs of my body quivering and my mouth drying up. In fact, my whole body is trembling, and my hair is standing on end. My bow is slipping from my hand, and my skin is burning.'"

There are also some aspects of the book and in the movie which have no relationship to the Gita; some even distort its principles and concepts. Nevertheless, if Bagger Vance awakens the interest in readers to take a closer look at the underlying, Bhagavad-gita, that is welcome. There is also another book that examines the connection between The Legend of Bagger Vance and Bhagavad-gita called Gita on the Green.

Bhagavad-gita is originally spoken in the Sanskrit language, but there are many translations in the West and also many interpretations. The most recognized and accepted (in scholarly circles, also) is a non-sectarian translation with the title Bhagavad gita As It Is, written by His Divine Grace Srila Prabhupada.

So many times during my tennis career, I was presented with imperfect knowledge and speculations. So many times, I was trying to implement all kinds of tips from various trainers and self-proclaimed experts, but they never brought tangible results in the matter of improving my performance.

For example, there were innumerable instructions how to position ones feet before the stroke, how to go low in the knees, how to move, and where to put the elbow of the striking arm during the backswing, etc. Sometimes, because it was a new instruction and I felt some enthusiasm about it, my attention increased. When this was the case, there was some short-term improvement. However, when the initial enthusiasm and excitement diminished, I went back to being the same player I was before. I then became aware that there was actually no improvement, and that the whole thing didn't work. It was disappointment after disappointment, and there appeared no end in sight to this cycle.

Study of the **Vedic** literature

The aforementioned Eastern books attracted me enormously. They came my way just at the right time. I immediately felt that this could make a difference; I believed that it was information coming to me from a completely different plane. I considered it solid knowledge and wisdom, the kind that does not change as did so many theories and speculations I had contacted in the past.

Vedic literature, <u>Bhagavad gita</u> being the part of it, is much bigger than sports, of course. I was still full of sportive desires, but I also had a desire to understand what was going on in life generally. I particularly wanted to know all of this in relation to my tennis game. At that time, my career as a tournament player was already diminishing, as I had almost no chance to practice tennis while serving in the army. Later, there was a chance—which I tried to exploit—when I worked for one of the clubs in Germany as a professional player and trainer.

The mystical personality Bagger Vance represents the Lord, Who is the main character in the <u>Gita</u>. He presents himself as an advanced esoteric person with unlimited knowledge, strength, and mystic power. His soft body is said to have a complexion of a blue cloud. Although His body looks similar to that of a human being— *as if* made of flesh and bone—it is completely spiritual.

He says that He is present in the heart of every living entity, and if somebody is interested, he can contact Him.

As my faith in these descriptions of the <u>Gita</u> grew, I began to imagine what it would look like if such a superior person like Krishna were playing tennis. There are descriptions of His activities in His worldly incarnations throughout the Vedic literature. He was a perfect archer, wrestler, and proved His unlimited skill and strength on innumerable occasions. As such, I imagined how weightless He moves, how softly He holds the racquet, and how His balls were hitting exactly the desired points on the court with greatest speed.

Mind is the nucleus of all bodily activities and changes. There have been many scientific experiments in this regard; I was impressed by the one presented in <u>Natural Health</u> (March, 1999 edition) written by Dave Smith, a sports psychology researcher at Manchester Metropolitan University in England. He gathered eighteen men and had six of them contract their pinkie fingers as hard as they could for twenty minutes a day, two times per week. Six others were instructed to just imagine themselves doing this exercise. The third (placebo) group did nothing at all. After thirty days, the pinkies of the first group were 33% stronger. Those of the third control group were unchanged. The men who visualized themselves doing pinkie crunches increased their finger strength by 16%!

Some **realizations** set into **practice**

My faith in the visualization process was strong. Simultaneously, I was thinking that there could not possibly be any better visualization objective than Krishna. In this treatise, I will occasionally call him either the Supreme Player or the Supreme Teacher. The narrations from <u>Bhagavad-gita</u> are presented as historical facts. The lesson learned from the Manchester University experiment, however, is this: Even if you are unable to consider the historical facts or you think everything about Krishna is myth, you will still get benefit if you seriously perform the suggested mental visualizations.

After I returned from Germany, I was engaged as a private trainer for a good young prospect whose name was Iztok. He was quick and a very good worker, despite being a little stiff. He was a few years younger than myself, and previously we traveled quite often together to various tournaments; I was still playing back then, so he was actually a co-competitor. Now, I became his trainer and not a competitor.

When standing courtside, I never talked more than necessary—and that was not much. When watching him practice, I always contemplated two persons: One being the person I was teaching (Iztok) and the other being Krishna. First, I imagined how Krishna, the Supreme Player, would hit the ball, and then I tried to bring my student to that standard. Without his knowledge, I gave the young man a perfect role model. It was just like painting a picture, adding a little here, subtracting a little there. As already mentioned, I restrained my speech as much as possible. Most of his transformation was accomplished by effort to focus concentration and will.

The most important thing I realized, through meditation on the Supreme Player, was that His stroke and movement represented perfect relaxation. He moved smoothly; He was holding the racquet very softly without pressure, and the racquet was weightless in his palm. There was no ball he could not reach, and there was no ball he would miss. It was soon clear to me, if I wanted to bring Iztok closer to that stage of relaxed moving and hitting, I would need to make some drastic changes in his training process.

It is my experience, throughout my teaching career, that students couldn't realize what I wanted when telling them to relax. You can hear almost every trainer — be it in tennis, golf, or any discipline — telling their students to relax. However, I hardly remember even one student who really understood and acted upon this crucial instruction.

There was significant stiffness in Iztok, so this was the first problem that needed attention. At first, he was a little unwilling to recognize this problem, but then he, somehow or other, trusted me; he was willing to cooperate. Just instructing him to relax was not at all enough. I insisted that he go to the extreme of learning the new feeling. I first designed a few exercises: Just shaking the body, bowing the body forward and letting the arms and shoulders swing freely and loosened. Then, I instructed him to imitate a drunkard. When a person is drunk, then he is usually very relaxed and uses only those muscles he really needs to function or to move.

We went on half court, and I showed him how to imitate a drunkard. We laughed and had fun doing this, but gradually he could understand what is actually wanted: **To use only those muscles that are necessary**. If unnecessary muscles are activated, then these will steal energy and eventually hinder the muscles that are needed. I wanted him to inwardly monitor the muscles, so that he became aware of the difference between the stiff and relaxed state. Long-term practice and continuous control of the muscles is necessary for changing from stiffness to relaxation, so this gradually became his second nature.

Besides continuous control (in order to make him relaxed), there was another thing that drew my attention. The way he stroked the ball, the sound of contact, and his effort in general was not compatible with my meditation on the Supreme Teacher. When the Supreme Player stroked the ball, it was completely effortless; the stroke seemed perfect, with the ball leaving the racquet at great speed, as if weightless. I concentrated on this, and I demanded it from Iztok. I avoided wordplay as much as possible, however. I did let him know what sound I wanted to hear from his strokes: The deep, relaxed bhamm, bhamm . . . He understood.

I realized that if we were to follow the usual training plan, the whole enterprise would not succeed. If we immediately jumped to so-called normal practice tempo, he would never be able to keep the relaxed state of his body and the correct sound of his shots. In this way, I insisted that we stay on half court (or, at most, three-quarters court), and I made no compromise here. Soon he felt that something good was happening, so he accepted my direction. Sometimes, we practiced in this way for the whole practice session, up to two hours. Of course, when he began to stabilize in the relaxed state and was able to hit the ball effortlessly, we then practiced tempo. Nevertheless, we never compromised the basic premise. If there was some stiffness creeping in or some other mistake, we immediately slowed down and went back to half court practice.

We had the opportunity to practice like this during the winter season; later there were tournaments. His progress was immense. He was more swift and flexible than before, his shots were effortless, precise, and powerful. Very soon, he became a successful ATP tour player — and the best player of our country for many years.

We had a great time practicing. However, as the saying goes, we are all like straws on the current of a river; sometimes the current of the river gathers the straws together, and then again, sometimes it separates them. We parted ways after a little more than a year of working together in these effective practice modules.

Experience with Monika Seles

Monika Seles originally came from Serbia, which was formerly part of Yugoslavia, as was Slovenia. As such, we were actually living in the same country at the time she decided to come to Slovenia in preparation for the tournament season. She chose a place in the mountains known for good skiing facilities, and there is a nice sports center with a hotel there. It has a few tennis courts and various opportunities for different sports and relaxation, such as cycling and similar pastimes.

She was at the top of her career at that time (she had won nine grand slams already), and she invited Iztok to play the role of her sparring partner, so to speak. I happened to be his trainer then, so I joined them for a week or so. She was there with her father, who remained her trainer from early childhood up to her world-class championship status. The hotel with the sports center was more or less empty at that time, so the atmosphere in general was peaceful and very conducive for tennis training.

Although the hotel was generally empty and nobody would bother her, it was not possible to see her in the hotel lobby hanging around the complex. She was either practicing or she was in her room. I never saw her wasting time. In the morning, she was practicing with her father and, in the afternoon, with Iztok. Her father was actually not playing with her; he was hitting the balls from a basket standing at the half court, and she was on the other side, sometimes at half court, sometimes on three-quarters court. The balls her father hit were relatively slow, and she was also hitting them back with only 20-50 percent of her power. However, she was completely concentrated: The strokes were executed with cent-pre-cent precision, their impact was clean. These strokes were not just slow playing but exact imitations of full power shots. Occasionally, she would increase the power in order to demonstrate her full potential, but not often.

In the afternoon, as aforementioned, she would practice tempo with Iztok. At that time, she hit the balls with full power. Although she missed a ball here and there, the precision rate relative to tempo was high. Her shots were powerful; she knew very well how to use the sweet spot on the racket. She probably knew how to use it from the very beginning. She was always the best player of our country in her category, and everyone wondered how such a small girl could play such powerful tennis. The training system she followed was good confirmation of the system that I had begun to develop while instructing Iztok.

Not long ago, I read about a great classical guitarist named John Williams. He is known for his outstanding and "perfect" technique, and his life story reminded me of Monika Seles. Williams was also thought by his father, who was reputed to be a great teacher. The junior Williams started at four, and he practiced very little, not more than half an hour daily. He was not allowed to practice unsupervised for a number of years; that means that he was not allowed to practice or play wrongly. He was not allowed to practice on his own until he was responsible enough to practice correctly.

The **sweet spot** of the racquet

While meditating inwardly on the Supreme Player, one thing particularly drew my attention: It was the moment when His racquet contacted the ball. This picture was a little hazy, so I devoted special attention to it. Gradually it became clearer and clearer, and I began to see two perpendicular lines in the frame of the racquet, intersecting exactly in the center. I saw His racquet contacting the ball at exact center every time. The whole meditation became much more satisfactory, and gradually I began to imagine this contact in slow motion. The racquet just touched the ball at the exact sweet spot and the ball came off weightless, with great speed. This soon became the essence of my contemplation.

I had been reading about the sweet spot a few times and heard some talk about it, also. However, I was not aware of its importance and never seriously considered that I needed to devote special attention to it, engaging in special training for this purpose. When I look back at the time I was a tournament player, I remember that the strings of my racquet were worn out mostly on the upper-half head of the racquet. This is not at all good. I will not go into some impractical details here regarding where the exact sweet spot is; if somebody is able to hit the ball constantly at the exact center of the racquet, he is activating the power of the sweet spot.

I was sure that the sweet spot was described in books. However, I didn't see any really consistent description that detailed all of the aspects that it influences—and how crucial it actually is. There are books that describe various aspects of the tennis game. For example, they talk about the importance of the correct forehand grip, how your elbow has to be in such position when you make a backswing, how your stance should be like this or like that. Then, in the same category, they tell you that there is a point on the racquet called the sweet spot, which transfers maximum power when hit properly. From such a description, a casual reader will think that all these instructions are of equal importance.

If he is a little more clever, he can see that there are many top players who differentiate themselves from one another regarding forehand grip. So, why should he stick very strictly to a particular forehand grip instruction from any one book? The same goes for the elbow, when making the forehand backswing—for the stance, as well. We can see all these variations out there, why should anyone stick to a particular one? In this way, an intelligent tennis player does not take these instructions all that seriously. He thinks that there is no harm if he does all of these a little in his own way, and he is right about that decision.

However, here is the associated problem of the instruction about the sweet spot of the racquet. Because it is presented in the same category as all of the other pointers, he will also not take it seriously. However, the fact is that point of impact is completely different in importance. It is essential! If one does not master it, he will hit the wall at a certain point and become despondent. Let us look at why point of impact is so important.

The first thing is that, when you hit the sweet spot, maximum energy is transferred to the ball, and the stroke feels effortless. Recently, I come across a funny but truthful thought: "... a ten-year-old girl hits the ball harder than the Governor of California if she hits the sweet spot and he doesn't! Yet players subscribe to the myth that hitting power is a function of muscle power." Hitting the sweet spot consistently for power is one thing, but there is another thing that is even more important: Control of the ball off the racket.

The most desirable thing is to consistently hit the ball precisely on the sweet spot. Every time the player contacts the ball in that way, he will get the same feeling and result. He will see the power and precision of flight with his ball. He will know what to expect, so trust in his shots will grow.

A medium effectiveness occurs when the ball is hit *near* the optimal point of impact but **always at the same spot**. The power of the shot will decrease, and, the direction of the ball's flight will change. However, a player can get accustomed to the feeling and direction derived from this, despite not taking advantage of optional impact.

The worst result is when the point of impact is uncontrolled and **changes** constantly. The power and direction of the ball's flight is changing unpredictably, although the player may think that he hits the ball the same way every time. He expects something, but something else actually happens. There is no way for him to develop trust in his shots. There is nothing very mystical about any of this; it's physics. When the ball is hit away from the sweet spot, it bounces from the strings with less power and the angle changes as well. There will also be forces that turn the racquet, if the ball is hit either to the right or left of the sweet spot. Most of the power is lost when the ball is hit close to or at the dead spot on the racquet, which lies above the sweet spot at the top of the racquet's head.

One may ask, what about slice and spin shots? Is it good to hit the ball exactly on the sweet spot also? The answer is in the affirmative. Of course, when hitting a strong slice or spin, the ball rolls over the strings a bit. When one hits a strong slice or spin shot, the ball rolls a little over the string-bed. So, it should touch the strings a little on one side of the sweet spot and then roll over the sweet spot and leave the strings a little on the other side of the sweet spot. When the ball is midway on the strings, it should be exactly on the sweet spot.

This is the point where most tennis players hit the wall and just cannot progress further. I am one who knows; this was the source of frustration for me in my youth. There are some rare players, some very special talents, who naturally develop the feeling and consistency of the sweet spot. Others, ninety-nine percent or more, have intrinsic problems with it, unless they consciously and systematically practice.

At this point you may ask: "Why are you going into such detail here regarding a tennis stroke? This book is supposed to be about golf!" The point is that the physics of impact in these two sports is more or less the same, as you will read later in this booklet. I describe these tennis realizations, because they were crucial to my later understanding of the golf swing.

Idea for the training aid

From my experience in teaching others, it is diffi-cult to work on improvement of point of impact by commonly-accepted practicing standards. The common way means a few minutes of warm up on half court, and then so-called normal training with tempo, hitting paral-lels, diagonals, volleys, etc. Improving the precision and consistency of point of impact is a difficult task and re-quires full attention. At least in the beginning, it cannot be mixed with other aspects of the game. A player must cut his regular training routine and reserve a period of time only for point-of-impact practice. Later, when he becomes consistent and comfortable with the correct point of impact, he can implement its practice into regu-lar training.

I already had experience of slowing down tempo and teaching the proper point of impact, emphasizing persistence and patience. Attention to the sound and feel of impact was stressed. However, this was not practical for the majority of the players. I was successful using this method to a considerable degree while working with Iztok, but he was a little different. His motivation was very strong, and he was a person with a powerful will and ability to concentrate. When he understood what we were actually doing, he stuck to it even while alone. We were practicing this 'proper feel and sound' discipline on half court, yet I occasionally saw him additionally practice this same thing against the wall, without my telling him. With other players, especially younger ones, I had much more difficulty. Their concentration was weaker; they were able to keep attention on proper impact for only a limited duration of time.

I began to look for an alternative, some effective training method that would increase awareness of the sweet spot. Meditation on the Supreme Teacher had played a crucial role in my thinking process. As described before, I imagined the contact of His racquet with the ball in slow motion, how He hit it exactly at the center. These thoughts resulted in a training aid without which I could not imagine how to teach anybody this art of the tennis stroke.

The sweet spot is actually much smaller than propagated by racket manufacturers. It is a very small point; manufacturers simply draw a bigger area that they consider is still acceptable. However, the smaller the spot on the strings one uses for his shots, the better control he will have.

I remember a sportscaster commenting how Roger Federer dominated his opponent with shots that were surgically precise. He meant that the winners landed just a few centimeters inside the court lines. What is the cause of this surgical precision? The cause is point of impact executed to surgical perfection. *This is the essence: The impact.* In golf, they call it "the moment of truth." The first target is when a player aims to hit the ball at the sweet spot. The second target is when he aims the ball at the desired spot on the court. If he is not precise regarding the first target, the chances to be precise regarding the second target are lost.

Let us go back to the training aid. It is used off the court, and the best way to install it is on a wooden column attached to a wall. Two or three of them can be installed simultaneously, at different heights for different shots.

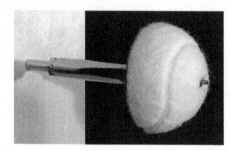

Picture 1. A removable housing that holds a ball with a pin that extends from the surface of the ball is affixed to the wooden column.

Picture 2. A removable small plate with a hole is affixed to the tennis racquet at its sweet spot and has a center hole of sufficient size to fit over the pin.

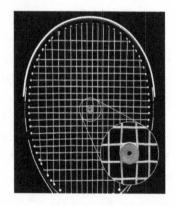

When practicing, a person imitates a normal full speed shot—forehand, backhand, volley, or service—and then precisely aligns the small hole on the pin that juts out of the ball and pushes it for a few centimeters. On the housing, there is a mechanism with a spring. As such, there is some resistance while pushing the ball; this is beneficial for timing and power at moment of impact.

How to **practice** with it

The main purpose of this practice method is to concentrate on, or draw awareness to, the racquet at one precise point: The center of the racquet, the sweet spot. One has to pay close attention to the pin that juts out of the ball, and, at the same time, feel the small hole (sweet spot) on the racquet as much as possible throughout the swing.

Then he tries to align the hole on the pin and pushes the ball for a few centimeters. A great deal of concentration and feeling is needed for this, and the consequence is that one feels the small hole more and more. After enough practice, when he then goes to the court, the plate with the small hole is not in the strings anymore—but he still feels it. In this way, he does not hit the ball with the head of the racquet but only with that phantom small hole, which is actually the sweet spot.

After enough practice, when he then goes to practice on the tennis court, it is much easier to concentrate on proper impact; awareness of the sweet spot becomes much sharper. I personally tested this method for some time and was amazed by my new perception of the game. The balls I stroke were so powerful, and everything seemed effortless. I realized that I missed the sweet spot practically my whole active tennis career. I now enjoyed every stroke more than ever. I always had problems with my backhand drive and spin, but now the return balls were deep and controlled. I can say that only then did I actually learn to enjoy tennis.

Later on, I began to work with an eleven-year old boy named Andrej. He was not the biggest or strongest amongst his contemporaries. He was regularly playing at a local club under the guidance of that club's trainers, but his father, wanting some additional practice for Andrej, asked me if I would help him. I offered to work with the boy on the training device I created, and, if there was time, on the court also.

Andrej was intelligent, and he understood well the meaning of practice on the training aid. However, there was one problem: He was very precise and concentrated when practicing on the device, aligning the small hole on the pin. When he played comrades at the club, however, there was chaos. He was young and forgot himself amongst other boys, who were all joking and competing at the same time. They would challenge each other as to who could hit harder. It was not pleasant to watch this nonsense.

However, we continued to work together for about a year; results were coming. When I practiced with him on the tennis court, I used exactly the same method I developed in the past. The main things were staunch persistence on relaxed playing and point of impact. From my experience, if I was able to really bring somebody to the relaxed state, then few additional instructions were needed regarding the stroke. When a person was relaxed enough, the body naturally found its best way to perform the stroke. Then there was, of course, point of impact. I always used my inner vision of the Supreme Teacher. If I was unsure of something, I compared the person I was teaching to my inner vision and immediately noticed problematic areas.

In the beginning of this booklet, I spoke how I was always changing my approach to the game. At one time something was important, and the next time something else. Most of the time, I was confused, simply trying to hit the ball as best I could. However, after I started to seriously study the whole thing, especially in conjunction with my study of the Vedic literature and the meditation process—learning from the Supreme Teacher whom I found in the <u>Bhagavad-gita</u>—I never changed methods again. My routine was the same throughout my teaching career, and it is the same today.

Andrej progressed with his game. We had a lot of fun practicing; his strokes were becoming more and more sharp and powerful. Soon, he became one of the best players in his category for our county. Our ways separated after about two years of cooperation. He was still very young at that time. Unfortunately, he eventually got lost in the ordinary club atmosphere that stymies systematic practice.

First **touch** with **golf**

Study of the Vedic literature, especially <u>Bhagavad-gita</u>, greatly helped me to better understand sports. However, Vedic study is much greater than sport; it includes all aspects of life. Gradually, I entered deeper and deeper into it, and my life changed dramatically. More and more, I desired to follow the spiritual path presented in that literature. There were tests. In the beginning, these tests were easy, but once I went up the road a ways, the tests became tougher and tougher.

At some point, I was confronted with a major test that was obviously a bridge too far, and I failed. Despite this, I traveled a few times to the East, but ultimately I came back. Now I found myself apparently trapped between two worlds. It became clear that I needed to make an accommodation for the time being. Upon returning from Germany, and after the aforementioned trips to the East, I became aloof from the sports scene. I was now at home in Slovenia, and I was an employee in my parents' family business. Additionally, for quite some time, problems in my back persisted. So even if I had wanted to engage in sports, it would have been more pain than enjoyment due to that affliction.

A new golf course had been designed in a city within close proximity, and my parents occasionally went there to play. They had clubs at home, so this was my first contact with golf. That was about twelve years ago. There are differences, of course, between tennis and golf—but there are also some common points. Quickly it became clear to me that the point of the game I had found essential to successful tennis is equally important in golf: The point of impact. It is even more important in golf, as all the running in tennis can compensate for many other disadvantages. In golf there is no movement like that; there is only the swing and the most important part of it, the impact. As in tennis, if you miss the sweet spot on the clubface, there will be loss of power and distance, as well as difference in the direction of the ball flight.

Implementation of the training aid for golf

In principle, the training aid that I created for tennis dovetailed well to golf, and I saw no reason that a modified version of it could not serve for perfecting golf practice. In a short span of time, I created the first prototype, and immediately after first tests, I was convinced about its efficacy.

I studied the golf scene and various teaching approaches for some years, but I could see that the training method I developed was and remains unique. As in the tennis community, there is not enough emphasis on the correct point of impact in golf; its importance is still largely underestimated.

Although there are training methods and aids that deal with optimal point of impact (the sweet spot), they are either impractical or just for mesuring the precision of the impact location. The difference between all these methods and aids and my method and training aid is basically this: They all require a swing at normal speed. Contrary to this, my training method and aid requires a slow motion swing, and this alone puts it on a completely different platform.

In my technique, all the back and forth swings are done in slow motion; it is only in this way that the golfer can stay relaxed, experience the whole motion in detail, and develop a perfect "groove" in his swing plane. These are just the first general indicators; detailed explanations follow.

Ben Hogans' teachings

Ben Hogan was one of the best golfers in the history of the game. Although he played more than fifty years ago, his teachings, his books, and his influence still dominate the world of golf. Hogan was known to practice more than his contemporaries and is even said to have "invented practice." Many aspiring golfers have studied his approach and books. As a result, they have developed their own theories about his swing and his teachings. Many golf aficionados speak of some special secret he was supposed to have revealed, however, there are some that say Hogan was actually a sly person, i.e., he did not actually want to reveal anything important.

That he may well have not given us his deepest realizations at some point is understandable. Just look at the competitive world around us. Not so long ago, there were lawsuits in Formula One circles because somebody was revealing technical secrets to a competitive team. No team wants to give out information; they want to use their secrets and discoveries to their own advantage. This is also the case with golf. Golf professionals will give out some general tips in magazines or to reporters, but the really important knowledge is considered a personal asset, helping them to maintain competitive edge. They don't reveal these techniques. If I was still active in tennis, either as a tournament player or a coach in the competitive environment, then it is almost certain that I would not have written this booklet for the very same reason.

My realization is that, over the course of time, Ben Hogan did actually reveal his secret knowledge, but he didn't serve it up on a silver platter. When he was asked about his chief secret, he mysteriously replied, "The secret is in the dirt." Many talk about his technique, about minute details concerning his stance, his grip, his backswing, etc. However, what was really special about him was that he was able to ingrain the swing so deeply into his sub consciousness that he could perform it with unmatched consistency and precision.

There were and remain many top golfers who employ a different swing than Hogan's, so I am sure that, even if Ben Hogan would today choose a slightly different swing style, he would still be able to program it to his great level of consistency and precision. The question is: What did he do that enabled him to ingrain his swing so perfectly? The ultimate question would be: How did he practice?

In his books, he speaks about fundamentals that every beginner should understand and work on. However, he admits that this is just A.B.C: "In these lessons, we will certainly not be attempting to cover all of golf or even one-hundredth of that almost inexhaustible subject." Five Lessons, The Modern Fundamentals of Golf

Not so long ago, a video of Ben Hogan appeared on the Internet, where he is seen showing his friends how he practiced. It is obvious that this footage was not meant for the broader public, however, after so much time, we can be thankful for its appearance. The movie was taken at Seminole Golf Club, in a backyard of one of his friends.

Golf instructor Chuck Evans comments on it:

> "As Hogan was getting set up, he kept directing the person shooting the video to move the camera so that it would be in the right place—teaching pros who use video take note!
>
> Once he was satisfied with the camera placement, he started waggling the club but in slow motion. Once the waggle was done, he started his backstroke—again in slow motion. Once he reached the top of the backstroke, he started the downstroke—again in slow motion, all of the way into impact, follow through, and finish.
>
> One of the ladies present at that time asks, 'Benny, why are swinging so slow?' Hogan replied, 'At this pace, I can control the golf club and everything in my swing. Whenever I am working on something, I always do it in slow motion. That way I can monitor what I am doing.'"

Please take a look at the excerpt of this recently published video on the following website: http://www.thesolarsweetspot.com/BenHogan

Picture 3. Snapshot from the footage of Ben Hogan
taken at the Seminole Golf Club

From the entire video, it is obvious that Hogan felt relaxed amongst his friends. He was already aged, and his heart had softened in this private atmosphere. He was willing to show his friends whatever they asked him.

In his books, he spoke about swinging in front of a mirror (without a ball) in order to shape the correct form of the swing. However, in the truest sense of the term, he never spoke about the slow motion practice presented in this video. On this basis, the video can be considered as a very important revelation concerning Ben Hogan's mysterious knowledge; there should be no doubt about this. On the assumption that you watched the video (as directed previously), you might have noticed another slow motion footage. It is an additional great piece of evidence related to Hogan's training methods. This footage is much older, however. At first glance, it seems that it is just a swing at normal speed in slow motion. However, notice the audience in the background!

Picture 4. Snapshot from much older footage of Ben Hogans' slow motion practice

It is amazing how smoothly and with such a flow he is able to conduct his swing in slow motion. At first glance, I was sure that this was just a slow motion movie. His slow motion swing is a perfect copy of the full speed swing. It is obvious that he practiced golf innumerable hours in this way.

The **correct** practice

The best practice methods are surprisingly coun-ter-intuitive to all except a few special and extraordinary minds. This is the main explanation for why wrong prac-tice methods are incorporated. For example, the majority of tennis players and teachers think that, in order to de-velop tempo, one just needs to beat the balls—and tempo will somehow appear. The majority are practicing like that! I have witnessed it first-hand during my youth. It is complete nonsense.

Let's say that you own a serial car, and you want to participate in a rally in order to race with it. Now, you need your car to be faster and stronger. Will you just go to some practice racetrack and drive as fast as possible, hoping that you will get faster? No. You will bring the car into a garage and work on special automotive details practically; in this way, you will make the car stronger and faster. When the car is finely-tuned and super-powered, then you will go to the racetrack and practice driving with speed. Parallels from this example can be drawn in relation to virtually any other sport.

The most important part of correct practice is in its understanding. Tools and exercises cannot be used properly without these understandings. For example, the essential part of correct practice is slow motion practice. The mind is very tricky, and, if the student is not fixed enough in his understanding, he will become victim of mental distractions and the desire to practice in fast motion will sprout in him too soon. Only when a student truly understands the reason for engaging in extremely slow practice with great attention, will he or she actually do it. Once a student experiences the results of practicing this way, he will not waste time practicing any other way due to this realization.

My initial understandings regarding precise slow practice were exclusively the result of my meditation on the Supreme Teacher. At that time, I was aware that slow motion practice was used for centuries in learning Eastern martial arts, but I was unaware of this method as per its applicability to other fields. I was not keenly interested in making research into this area, as well. When I initially taught tennis, I had enough authority and reputation as a player and trainer so that my students were doing whatever I told them. I didn't need to bring in too much outside authority to convince them about my training methods and knowledge.

However, this changed dramatically when I transferred the slow motion training method to golf. I became very enthusiastic and interested to find out more about slow motion practice in general. I began to widely research everything in connection to this subject, and the cream of this research is presented in the next sections of this booklet.

Step by step process

One of today's top golfers is Padraig Harrington. He says that, when you play golf, you should leave the thoughts of technical details concerning your swing off the course and concentrate hundred percent on the target, where you want to hit the ball. Technique is for the practice range; on the course one should play the game. One should know how to play before getting on the course. Harrington says that he personally rarely thinks about technique on the course. When he fires different shots, all adjustments in his swing happen automatically.

This is similar to shooting a gun. When one goes to shoot a handgun or rifle, he will concentrate fully on the target. The firearm must be working properly in order to take advantage of it. One can concentrate on the target as much as he wants, but he does not control the bullet. The bullet will go its own way if the weapon is ram-shackled. Similarly, concentration on the target will not help the golfer if his swing is flawed. As such, before he goes on the course, he should have practiced enough to trust his swing; he should be practiced to the point that he does not need to think about it anymore. Then he can direct his concentration fully on the pin or on an area of the fairway.

This sounds easy, granted, but we all know that to master the swing is not an easy task. The perfect swing must become second nature. Actually, it seems to many people that this is an impossible task. That is mostly because of bad practice habits.

Ben Hogan has nicely explained the bare fundamentals of the swing and how to practice them in his book <u>Five Lessons: The Modern Fundamentals of Golf</u>. There are many other books that describe these basics, so we will not go into all of that in this booklet. I will assume that you are already aware of the fundamentals: The correct grip, stance, backswing, downswing, and follow through. When practicing these fundamentals, do not keep too many words in your head. Pictures are much more effective. First, you should see it; then feel it. After that, do it (see it, feel it, do it). This is where practice comes in.

In the forthcoming analysis, I want to bring your special attention to the following two essentials:

- **Proper relaxation**
- **Point of impact**

These two essentials are universal factors in all sports that have anything to do with striking a ball.

Proper **relaxation**

The big obstacle in learning any physical skill—be it tennis, golf, playing piano, guitar, or dancing—is unnecessary muscle tension. It has to be eliminated, and the first step in doing so (as in solving any problem) is to become aware of it. Until you become aware of your muscle tension, you can make certain movements millions of times, but nothing will change. The more you try, the more the tension and frustration will increase.

There is the example of a child who has his shoelaces tied together: He will learn to walk somewhat—with a lot of trouble—but he will never be able to run. This is how we do things, but we must become aware of the muscle tension problem and consciously rectify it. When I was teaching tennis, I do not remember even one beginning student who had proper relaxation.

In many cases, my students didn't like my persistence in this matter; they felt I was a bit weird about it. They were not accustomed to any of this; the new feeling was unnatural. Nevertheless, I was strict about it; I would not continue with them if they didn't want to relax. It is painful to watch somebody suffer on the court due to muscle tension.

It is a fact that, with proper practice, just about anything will begin to feel natural, in due course of time. When I began to practice the golf swing, I gripped the club just as I would grip a tennis racquet. This felt natural for me. However, later I had problems at the top of my swing, so I learned the proper golf grip. In the beginning, it felt terrible. My left thumb under the right palm . . . this felt weird and unnatural. However, today the feeling is just the opposite. If I would now grip the club as I had in the beginning, *that* would feel terrible. With correct practice, you can make almost anything second nature.

Proper relaxation, as already mentioned in previous chapters, is the ability to use only those muscles you need for particular movement. Additionally, it means that you relax the muscles as soon as they do their part of the job. Shoulders should be the object of special attention. Thus, you can work as hard as you want and still be relaxed.

Muscle tension means that you activate muscles that work at cross-purposes in regard to particular movement. Unnecessary activated muscles hinder the necessary muscles. For example, in the golf swing, too tight of a grip will produce tension in your arms and shoulders. This will impede speed, free flow, and the smoothness of the swing. In the video (abovementioned), Ben Hogan explains the pressure points on the grip. "There isn't any pressure down or around the shaft . . ." he says. Clearly, this shows how one should not squeeze the club—just push it.

One needs to feel the club head during the swing as much as possible, but this is hindered if there are any points of unnecessary muscle tension in the body. We grip the club with the fingers and try to feel everything that happens to the club. Impulses from our fingers travel through our hands and shoulders to our brains, but if there are points of muscle tension on the way, these impulses reach the brain in a blurred state; our awareness gets bollixed up in these stress points. In this way, the sense of feel in the awareness of the critical moving object, the club head, is significantly reduced.

> "Muscular freedom is probably more important in golf than in any other sport, but very few players take the trouble to get loosened up." Ben Hogan, *Power Golf*

You might think that you are relaxed enough, however, if you didn't devote special attention to this point—or didn't undergo some special training in this area—then take it from me, you are not.

Being able to look inside and monitor the critical parts of the body in order to keep the muscles relaxed is mandatory. This can be best practiced in slow motion. One cannot progress with unnecessary muscle tension, and this is a universal principle that applies to any physical skill. When you begin to practice the swing, always conduct some relaxation exercises, like shaking arms and shoulders, legs, and body. Just to get acquainted with the feeling, make a few swings (without a ball) imitating a drunkard, as I had taught my tennis students. The example of a drunkard may be a little tasteless, but this visualization worked well for them. I do not know of any other example that would so obviously communicate what is actually wanted here. So, if you are not averse to the imagery, use this visualization, as it will help you to achieve the state of desired muscle relaxation.

While doing these exercises, carefully monitor for possible tension in your hands, arms, shoulders, back, hips, legs, and whole body. Of course, it is not possible to execute the swing properly in such a state, so, when you feel relaxed enough, carefully begin to activate only those muscles you really need for swinging the club precisely. With this muscle set, while eliminating the interference from unnecessary muscles, you should find that you actually need much less energy for the swing than you thought.

As abovementioned, two essential points are stressed in this booklet. The second point is dependent on the first one. In this way, I cannot stress enough how important it is for you to eliminate unnecessary muscle tension and relax properly every time you practice.

Point of **Impact**

Point of impact is the most important part of the swing; it decides where the ball will land. Swing mechanics is there just to facilitate point of impact. Usually it is assumed that, if you learn the fundamentals—like proper stance, grip, turning of hips, etc.—you will somehow automatically become expert at point of impact. Proper fundamentals are a good basis, but, in most cases, not at all enough for precision. How easy it is to miss the optimal swing path by half of an inch at impact! The precision is then lost, despite correct fundamentals and an apparently perfect swing.

Sometimes, when we visited international tennis tournaments, there were many players who we didn't know. In this way, we contemplated them, mostly before the tournament started; we looked at how they practiced. There were so many wrong judgments about who was actually a good player. So many different styles were on display. Sometimes, somebody looked less than average, but then it turned out that he was one of the leading players. The point is that style is not important. What is important is how one is able to strike the ball when it touches the strings, especially when the game gets tough. The same thing goes for golf. In the introduction to his recent book _The Impact Zone: Mastering Golf's Moment of Truth_, Bobby Clampett writes:

"You've probably heard that the most important six inches in golf is between the ears. Though the mind unquestionably plays a key role in the game, the most important six inches in the swing truly take place through the Impact Zone — meaning the two inches before impact through the four inches after it. After all, they don't call impact the golf swing's Moment of Truth for no reason."

To hit the ball on the sweet spot is the basis of everything, but there is a common misconception about it created by the manufacturers of golf clubs. They call the sweet spot a certain area around the actual sweet spot:

"First, the sweet spot isn't an area of the clubface; it's actually a pinpoint on the strike area where the CG (center of gravity) is optimized. Manufacturers can't really increase the size of the sweet spot, but they can increase the forgiveness of the area around it by using variable face thicknesses, increased perimeter weighting and back weighting—elements made possible by increased head volume." Lana Ortega, LPGA

The manufacturers can make the area around the sweet spot more forgiving but never the same as the actual sweet spot. No doubt, the precision through the impact zone is crucial and has to be practiced with great attention.

Avoid mistakes while practicing

Here are the well-known words of Earl Woods, Tiger's late Father: "Practice makes permanent; Perfect Practice makes perfect." The essence of practicing the swing is that we hit the ball on the correct swing path, with the correct clubface angle, and exactly on the sweet spot every time. How can we practice such a perfect swing if we are not able to perform it in the first place? Answer: **slow it down!**

This is the way many great masters and teachers recommend we learn things, and this is the way they learned it. It has been used for centuries in martial arts, in fencing, and, in the post-modern era, in a variety of sports. We can find the slow motion practice method used by great performers in the world of music, such as pianists, violinists, guitarists, and other musicians. There is an interesting statement made by Ben Hogan about practicing piano in his book <u>Five Lessons</u>:

> "Learning the grip and stance and posture clearly and well is, in a way, like having to practice the scales when you're taking up the piano. In fact, the more I think about it, the best way to learn golf is a great deal like learning to play the piano: you practice a few things daily, you arrive at a solid foundation, and then you go on to practice a

few more advanced things daily, continually increasing your skill."

It is obvious that Ben Hogan knew something
about practicing piano. Let us, therefore, take a glimpse
into the world of piano practice. Although I found many
examples of slow practice in the piano world, one book
particularly impressed me. It is <u>Fundamentals of Piano
Practice</u> by Chuan C. Chang. He stresses precision in
slow practice:

> "In order to memorize well, and to be able to play
> fast, you must practice slowly, even after you can
> play the piece easily at speed. This is counter-
> intuitive because you always perform at speed, so
> why practice slowly and waste so much time?
> Since you perform at speed, you would think that
> practicing at speed will help you to memorize
> and perform it well. It turns out that playing fast
> can be detrimental to technique as well as to
> memory."

He continues:

> "Therefore, although much of this book is orient-
> ed towards learning to play at the correct speed,
> it is the proper use of slow play that is critical in
> achieving the goals of strong memorization and
> performing without mistakes. However, practic-

ing slowly is tricky because **you should not practice slowly until you can play fast!** Otherwise, you would have no idea if your slow play motion is right or wrong . . . It is important, when playing slowly, to maintain the same motion as when playing fast."

The last two sentences are interesting in comparison to Ben Hogan's advice:

"My advice to the beginning golfer is to go ahead and hit the ball as hard as he can right from the start. He will be wild for a time. That's only natural. Later on he can straighten out his hooks and slices with minor alterations to his swing. But if he doesn't learn to hit the ball hard right at the start, he will never be able to get distance without a major overhauling, because his speed and timing setup will be something less than his full power."

Hogan's advice to a beginning golfer is to begin his swing practice before a mirror, slowly. However, before that, he should get some idea how to swing at full speed. He should know and understand the correct swing before he starts slow motion practice, which will ingrain that movement into the sub-consciousness. Otherwise, if he practices wrongly, a radical overhaul will be necessary later.

This is the same thing Chang is saying about piano practice. One has to know the correct movements of hands and fingers by slow practice before he begins to ingrain them into his brain. Slow motion practice is not simply slow playing, as slow motion running is not walking. It is the exact copy of running, but running motions are conducted slowly. Similarly, the slow motion swing is the exact copy of the full speed swing.

There was a practice technique used by Wolfgang Amadeus Mozart, which he learned from his father, Leopold. The elder Mozart would place ten dried peas in his son's left coat pocket, and for each successful attempt at a difficult passage, Mozart would move a single pea to his right pocket. When he failed on any piece, even if it was the tenth repetition, all the peas had to be placed back in his left pocket; he had to begin anew. What generally happens when using this method is that a student slows down his tempo in order to play the passage perfectly.

There is a very similar practice method presented by world-class clarinetist Daniel Bonade:

> "Practice and performance are completely different. **All** practice must be slow until the passage is perfect. The formula is 9 + 1 x 10. That is, you perfect a passage so that you can play it nine times perfectly at 1/10 the final speed. Then play it one time perfectly at performance speed. (If all ten repetitions are not perfect, start again). Repeat

the 9 + 1 pattern ten times perfectly before you put the passage away as well-mastered."

Crucial to this process is avoiding mistakes while practicing. As the saying goes, "If you do it wrong three times, you own it!"

It is said that for every repetition required to learn a pattern of motion, it takes seven times that number of repetitions to change the pattern. If you notice errors during your practice, stop. Review what you are doing and further reduce the speed of your motions.

Post Practice Improvement (PPI)

There is another principle mentioned in Chang's piano book called post practice improvement (PPI). When you practice, you may not notice any improvement; you may become doubtful that you are making progress. Chang says that the practice session is conditioning, and the real progress actually takes place after the practice session, while resting. This is the time when muscle and nerve cells grow. There is the example of a body builder who actually looses weight while he practices; his muscles do not grow at that time. However, during the following hours, his body will react to the tearing stimulus and add muscle. Almost all real muscle growth happens after weightlifting. The body builder does not measure how much muscle he gained, or how much more weight he lifted, at the end of an exercise. Instead, he concentrates on whether the exercise produced appropriate conditioning. Of course, while playing piano or practicing golf, one aims to develop much finer muscle and nerve cells in comparison to a body builder. Nevertheless, the principle regarding PPI is the same.

A similar example is when a person begins running. If you have not run for years, you may only be able to run for a quarter mile before you need to slow down. After some rest, if you try to run again, you will tire out in a quarter mile or less. Thus, the first run resulted in no discernible improvement. However, the next day, you may be able to run a third of a mile before tiring—this is PPI. Chang says the most PPI occurs during sleep. This is because most cell growth and repair occurs during sleep. That is why babies and young children need so much sleep—they are growing rapidly.

One should be aware that post practice improvement **does** occur between two practice sessions if a person practices correctly. It may only be a small change. However, the cumulative effect of this occurring over weeks, months, or years can be huge and most beneficial.

Practice **Slow** To Learn **Fast**

We all tend to become impatient when making slow progress. There is no question of playing too fast too soon; that significantly hinders us. As golfers, it greatly increases the amount of time it will take for us to become precise and consistent strikers.

It is thrilling to watch those long precise shots. Naturally, we want to be able to play that way ourselves. Many of us impatiently play over our heads and unconsciously reinforce habits of poor play. What is the point of hitting the ball hard over and over while making mistake after mistake? It is a short-sighted and self-defeating strategy.

Do you remember the allegory of the tortoise and the hare? It's moral should be known to everybody.

However, the following allegory may be more applicable. Let's say that Mr. Hasty and Mr. Deliberate are beginning to build their own houses. Mr. Hasty does everything rashly, without much thought. He does not care for static measurements, he is negligent regarding proper isolation of the walls, etc. However, he makes quick progress in construction, and after six months he can sleep in his house. On the other side, Mr. Deliberate builds his house systematically and carefully considers all the aspects for building a safe, economical, and comfortable house. He finishes it in twelve months.

Now, after six months, Mr. Hasty is in a better position, since he can sleep in his house. Mr. Deliberate's house is still under construction, and he cannot enjoy it. However, after twelve months, Mr. Deliberate finishes his house, and he moves in at that time. It is very comfortable, safe and economical, and he especially enjoys living in it. On the other hand, Mr. Hasty is now dissatisfied with his house. He has large heating bills due to bad isolation, and when there is a strong wind, he feels as if his house will tear apart and fall on him.

A golfer who immediately begins with power shots on the training range may initially gain some advantage over the golfer who begins with slow practice. However, at some point, the power-hitter will hit the wall, and there will be no further progress for him in mastering the game of golf. On the other hand, the golfer who practices systematically, precisely, and solidly builds on the foundation of the basics suggested in this booklet, will be able to reach far beyond the limits of any hitter who follows Mr. Hasty.

The process of **"muscle memory"**

We all know the aphorism: "Easier said than done." It is no problem to intellectually consider a precise golf swing, yet it can take a very long time to gain the needed muscle skills for its fine performance. Research in biology, anatomy, and neurology is addressing this problem of muscle development. It is both intriguing and reassuring to know that, during a long learning period, you are literally building new nerve pathways that will become persistent and reliable. What follows is a somewhat technical explanation found in Grey Larsen's book _The Essential Tin Whistle Toolbox_, as written by Lawrence Washington, a musician and molecular biologist:

> "As we first start learning a new group of movements, such as the fingering motions used to execute a G long roll, we have to think consciously about each component of the group and command the muscles to move. The part of the brain responsible for conscious thought (the cerebral cortex) sends impulses through the muscle-control part of the brain (the cerebellum) and onward to the finger muscles. Since there are so many different, very precise muscle movements in a long roll, its execution is at first slow and tedious, requiring great concentration. The thought process may go something like this: 'Do a G long

roll: (1) place T1, T2, T3 on their holes, (2) blow, (3) lift T2, (4) replace quickly, (5) raise B1 high, (6) bring B1 down sharply...' and so on, all the while keeping the proper timing, breathing, and a raft of other elements in mind. There is so much to think about that it is no wonder we can feel overwhelmed and frustrated."

If we translate this to golf swing, it would read as follows:

As we first start learning a new movement, such as the golf swing, we have to think consciously about each component of the swing and command the muscles to move accordingly. The part of the brain responsible for conscious thought (the cerebral cortex) sends impulses through the muscle-control part of the brain (the cerebellum) and onward to the muscles. Since there are so many different, very precise muscle movements in the golf swing, its execution is at first slow and tedious, requiring great concentration. The thought process may go something like this: 'To execute a swing: (1) secure the stance, (2) grip the club, (3) address the ball, (4) begin with the backswing, (5) shift weight to the right foot, (6) turn your shoulders ...' and so on, all the while keeping the proper timing, breathing, and a raft of other elements in mind. There is so much to think about, that it is no wonder we may feel overwhelmed and frustrated.

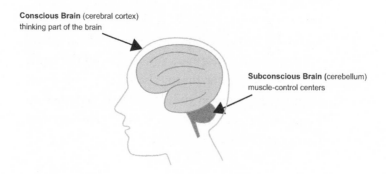

Picture 5. Functions of various parts of the brain.

Washington continues:

> "But there is good news to be found in the biology of learning. When we repeat a complex set of muscle motions, specific patterns of nerve pathways are assigned to repeat them. Gradually the muscle commands, which originate from the thinking part of the brain, the cerebral cortex, are taken over directly by the muscle-control centers of the cerebellum, which previously had only mediated them. All that remains at the conscious level is the initiating command: 'Do a G roll" ("*Execute a swing,*' or, '*Hit the ball*'). With that, the cerebellum takes over and commands all the individual movements, which we had to think about one by one when we were first learning. It is as though we have gradually built a very spe-

cific machine and now only have to flip a switch for that machine to do its job."

The frequency with which the pattern of movements is repeated in the same way, the stronger our neural pathways are established. The nerve connections become stronger, just as, to use the analogy employed by Washington, a beaten path through the woods becomes better defined the more times a herd of deer tramples over it.

If we practice wrong movements, our neural pathways will establish those. We should only practice what we want our muscles to learn. Having created wrong pathways and movements, it is more difficult to come to a right golf swing than if we were beginning from scratch.

> "Fortunately for the beginner, it does not matter that we execute movement patterns slowly as we learn them. After the neuronal pathways have established their circuits, we can go as fast as our muscles can move. The family of deer walking many times the same way through the woods clears a nice trace. Later they can run as fast as they like down the smooth trail, gracefully as a perfectly timed roll. And the established neural pathway is amazingly persistent. Once made, the additional synapses (a junction between two nerve cells) and increased density of nerve

branches stay. We may easily forget how to describe the details of a roll, but the nerves in our brain and fingers have made very strong connections that can be activated anytime we 'flip the switch.'" _The Essential Tin Whistle Toolbox_, Chapter 15 (Content in parentheses has been added)

This explanation is worth studying; I recommend you read through it at least four times. It will fix your intelligence in proper understanding by doing so. The movements have to be practiced with one-hundred percent precision. To be able to practice that precisely, you must slow down. Slow motion practice will establish specific patterns of nerve pathways (in due course of time), and then the golf swing can be conducted with speed and power.

Link between Ben Hogan's **mirror** practice and his **slow motion** drill

Ben Hogan divided the fundamentals of his golf swing into grip, stance and posture, the first part of the swing, and the second part of the swing. He proposed that a beginner learns these fundamentals in front of a big mirror. In his book he assumed that a golfer who followed these directions would gradually develop a swing that would automatically lead to crisp impact.[1]

The next drill Hogan wonderfully demonstrated was the slow motion drill presented in the abovementioned videos previously presented. This is a great drill, and I think that the post-modern outlook on slow motion practice will drastically change after the recent release of these long hidden films.

---

[1] Studies have shown that the majority of golfers just cannot hit the sweet spot, although going through various teaching programs and knowing these fundamentals. A group of fifty golfers were tested; they had handicaps of ten and above. It came out that they were able to make solid contact every fifth or sixth shot, i.e., by accident. On average, they missed the sweet spot by three-fourths (3/4") of an inch. (Tests made by Power Golf Academy by John Darling)

There are golfers who think that slow motion practice will make their swing slow. The answer to that doubt is this: If you practice in slow motion *with the proper mental attitude*, then this will never be the result. The final outcome will be just the opposite; your swing will be more precise, sharper, and more powerful. Correct slow motion practice will accumulate energy. Just see Hogan while he performs his drill, especially in the video of him when he was younger. How concentrated he is, and how precise and smoothly he conducts his slow swing. His attitude is just like that of a Shoalin monk conducting slow motion martial arts practice. They say that, with proper slow practice, the flow of chi energy increases. Professional musicians say, "Practice slow in order to play fast."

Imagine that you sit on a chair and are fanning yourself with a folding fan. Your hand moves slowly while moving the fan. Now imagine that you are sitting on a chair and, in one hand, you hold a needle. In the other hand, you hold a piece of a thread or a thin wire. In this exercise, you are continually trying to perfectly pierce the small hole of a needle. You are so fully concentrated on the small hole and on the point of the wire that you feel pins and needles throughout your whole body. Superficially, in both scenes, the right arm is moving slowly. However, there is a dramatic difference in the inner state of mind and awareness between these activities.

In the first visualization, I can sit without attention and fan myself. In this way, I will certainly not increase my ability to concentrate. In the second visualization, it is a completely different story. My concentration will have to increase, and my body will brim with energy if I practice like this regularly for any period of time.

In light of these two examples, if somebody practices the slow motion swing with a mental attitude of fanning himself, that will be a waste of time. Very soon, that person will find such practice boring and useless. However, if a person conducts the slow golf swing with a mental attitude like the second visualization, he will see very positive effects as a result of its discipline.

Additionally, tension is the enemy of speed. If you are performing a swing with tension in your arms and shoulders, there will be loss of swing speed. It is much like driving around with your parking brake on. You cannot drive fast and can even do some damage. If you do your swing slowly, you can work on *relaxing the antagonistic muscles* permitting free and fast movement. Once you are fixed in performing the movement smoothly in a slow manner, speeding it up is easy.

Even if an unaccomplished golfer performs Ben Hogan's slow motion drill with concentration, there will still be room for error. He makes a slow, precise, and smooth backswing, a similar downswing, and then he hits the ball and makes a smooth follow through. During such a slow swing, he tries to precisely stay on the correct swing path with the club head, maintaining proper angle of clubface. However, a person can still easily go off track at point of impact by ten or fifteen millimeters. Golf requires great precision. If we practice without due diligence—and the point of impact is off ten millimeters here, ten millimeters there—how can we expect a perfect swing with speed, power, and straight distance in the flight of the ball?

Referring to the previous section regarding "muscle memory," with practice we actually build a machine. At impact, **every millimeter counts**. However, if we are negligent about these millimeters while practicing, **we build a machine that will also be similarly negligent**. In that case, when we need exact precision, the machine will **not provide it to us, because we did not build it that way**. This lack of precision at impact is the reason golfers hit the wall at a certain point—and just can't make any further progress. As soon as one hits the ball off the sweet spot, there will be loss of distance and change of direction in its flight.

There is an aphorism: **"Genius is the ability to pay attention to details."**

This is the point where my golf training aid, developed for this very purpose, facilitates the method I have described here. It fits, as an essential step, between Ben Hogan's mirror practice and the slow motion drill.

Practice **method** facilitated by **training aid**

The main point of this training method is to practice a precise backswing, downswing, and, most importantly, an **EXACT** point of impact. It forces a golfer to 'hit' the ball on the sweet spot every time, and, simultaneously, he monitors the correct angle of the clubface.

An important part of this training method is that all the movements are practiced in slow motion. This applies equally to the backswing, as well as the downswing. That means the golfer first makes a slow and full backswing, then he starts the downswing. He moves the clubface slowly toward the ball and precisely targets the small hole on the pin that juts out of the ball. This is the fundamental technique for beginning exercises.

Picture 6. The slow motion swing should
be exact copy of the actual swing. Great precision
and concentration is needed for aligning the small hole on
the pin without hitting the border of the hole. There is only 1 mm
difference between the diameter of the hole and the diameter of the pin.

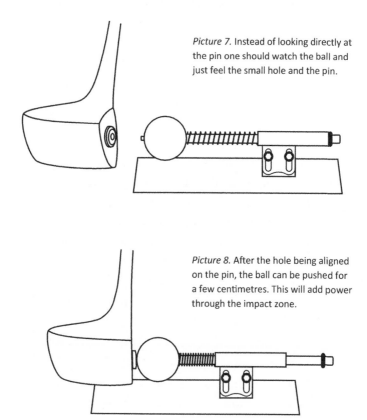

Picture 7. Instead of looking directly at the pin one should watch the ball and just feel the small hole and the pin.

Picture 8. After the hole being aligned on the pin, the ball can be pushed for a few centimetres. This will add power through the impact zone.

After a few training sessions and practice, the ball can be additionally pushed. You should then push it straight in the direction of the shaft, otherwise the shaft will serve as a block.

A great deal of concentration and feeling is needed in order to align the small hole on the pin. The consequence of doing this correctly is that a golfer's attention is continually drawn to that special place. After enough practice, he precisely feels the correct position of the club face (sweet spot) in relation to the ball.

The following quote gives an excellent description of the process, in relation to an increasing awareness to detail:

> "Imagine a light in a dark forest that illumines equally all objects within its range. If, by use of reflectors, that light is focused into a beam, the objects in the line of that beam will be seen in much sharper detail than previously, while those lying outside it will become less distinct. The relationship between awareness and attention is analogous. A human being's range of experience is made knowable by the light of his awareness, and is heightened selectively by the choices he makes in focusing his attention. That which we attend to we come to know. If we want to know something more closely--because we want to gain a greater measure of control or simply to appreciate it more--we need to shed more light on it by focusing our attention." The Inner Game of Golf (Timothy Gallwey)

In order to increase your awareness of a certain detail (point of impact in this case), you have to continually direct your attention on it—the more intensely and for longer periods, the better. It is the function of this training aid to help you in this essential process.

Some **tips** for **practicing** on the device

Level 1

1. Before you begin, relax your body, especially arms and shoulders. Always monitor to see if there is some unnecessary tension creeping in while practicing; at least have some awareness of it. Relax with every swing;

2. Ben Hogan introduced the idea of a plane of glass extending from the ball to his shoulders. Move the club head (or, to be more precise, the small hole, the sweet spot) on that imaginary plane, as if you are about to engrave a path **slowly** and **precisely** into the glass;

Picture *9*. Swing plane

3. Be careful to maintain the correct body position at the most important moment: IMPACT. See *Picture 6* above for reference. **Push the ball with the whole body, not just with the arms!**

4. In the beginning, watch the pin throughout the whole swing, especially when you align it to the small hole. Later, after a month or so of daily practice, **stop looking at the pin**. Simply look at the top of the ball (or its logo) and just *feel* the pin. Feel (be aware of) the pin and the small hole simultaneously throughout the swing, especially when you align the ball to the small hole. It is important to stop looking at the pin, because, when striking the ball normally, that is not what you will be doing;

5. **"And, in the end, the love you take is equal to the love you make." <u>Abbey Road</u>, The Beatles.** As much as you devote to practice, that much you will get out of it. The more you concentrate and try to align the small hole on the pin— **without hitting the borders of the hole**—the better conditioning you will achieve. Do this as slowly as practicable—but concentrate intensely, so that you feel pins and needles in your feet, legs, and whole body;

6. I recommend you to make slow swings and precisely align the small hole on the pin 75% of your practice time, without pushing it. The other 25%, you should additionally push the ball. Be careful not to squeeze the grip; just push the club very deliberately, that's all.

Picture 10. The small hole is precisely aligned on the pin.

You can practice as much as you want. However, if you notice that your concentration has decreased and errors have crept back in, **STOP!** Just as discipline is important for regular practice, **the discipline to know when to stop is just as important!** Remember, you do not want to ingrain wrong or imprecise movements into your swing.

I recommend that you secure a camcorder and occasionally use it to record your swing; almost all digital cameras can serve the same purpose. Utilize these great tools for evaluating your mechanics. Make a comparative analysis of your swing to the swing demonstrated by Ben Hogan; you can also access the swings of accomplished modern-day golfers from Youtube or other INTERNET sites. Once you record your swing and analyze it in this comparative way, you will, without doubt, discover adjustments that you need to make.

If you are a serious recreational or amateur golfer, the **minimum** slow motion practice on the device that I recommend is daily 3 x (2 x 25) swings. For example, you start in the morning, and the next fifty swings you make during the day. Then the last series of fifty swings (in slow motion) are made in the evening.

This practice should then be **combined with Ben Hogan's slow motion drill** as shown in the previously presented videos. Remember: **See it, Feel it, Do it.** While practicing this drill, try to be as precise as possible at the impact point—as precise as you were when aligning the small hole on the pin. Bonade's 9 + 1 x 10 practice system can be useful here. Nine slow swings—and then one with some speed. A deliberate choice of practice speed, alternating between slow and fast practice, is what enables you to optimize effectiveness.

When you swing with added speed, **think impact!** If you feel that you still need to think about technique during the swing, you are not ready yet for a swing with speed: Return to your slow motion practice regime.

Level 2

Harrington exemplifies the highest level of mastery; he makes exact impact both automatically and completely. In the same way, you must also develop full concentration on the real target: The spot where you want your ball to land in the fairway.

As mentioned before, he concentrates only on the target. When he plays different shots, all adjustments in his swing happen automatically. So, after we devoted enough time and concentration to the point of impact while practicing on the device, when we achieve a good percentage of alignments on the pin without hitting the border of the hole, it is time that we go to the next level, and that is full concentration on the target.

Now, from outside, exercising on the device looks the same, however, there is a big difference inside, namely where our attention or concentration lies. Now it should be directed **on the target**. That means, for example, that we imagine a hole with a flag in it 250 yards away, and then fully concentrate on it during practice. Aligning the small hole on the pin should, of course, still be very precise and, **automatic**. This is now a completely new filling and after mastering it, it will then be much easier to implement this technique when doing Hogan's slow motion drill with the ball and later on the course.

The more you repeat the pattern of movements, the more strongly the neural-linguistic pattern becomes established. This is a process that takes a long time, so you should **not measure your progress in terms of a few weeks or a few months**; measure it in terms of a longer period.

To be able to endure correct practice, you will need a lot of patience and a cool head. You can print out some of the thoughts and citations from this book and review them—speak them to yourself—while practicing. They will remind you of principles used by great masters. For example, consider the following piece of wisdom. It was offered by one of the most influential musicians of his time: Pianist, composer, author, and teacher, W. A. Mathieu:

> "You cannot achieve speed by speedy practice. The only way to get fast is to be deep, wide awake, and slow ... Pray for the patience of a stonecutter ... Pray to understand that speed is one of those things you have to give up - like love - before it comes flying to you through the back window."

Epilogue

Old wisdom says that man's talent can be compared to a treasure buried in a courtyard. There may be big treasure; there may be smaller treasure. However, simply having a treasure buried in a courtyard does not help a person: It must be located and dug up! So, whatever golf potential you have buried in yourself, the knowledge and the method presented in this book can help you to bring it out. The training aid is essential, also.

Along with attention, if you devote significant effort to learning and using the principles presented in this book, you will surely see continual improvement of your golf striking ability.

It gets a little complicated when competition is involved, of course. I remember an interview with former tennis star Boris Becker. He was questioned after a difficult match, and he explained his experience during the most crucial moments. He said that he felt completely lost at a certain point; there was nothing he could do. He was helpless. Then, almost out of nowhere, his shots became precise and powerful. He said that all he was doing at that time was observing the process as a whole. He said that, when he did that, he felt somebody up there liked him. He won the match, of course.

It is obvious that he pointed to some higher power, and the Highest Power is God, the Supreme Player. Why would God favor him over his opponent? What if his opponent also prayed to God for victory? According to Vedic wisdom, the Supreme Player rarely interferes in mundane activities like sporting contests; He leaves the whole affair to the law of karma. According to the law of karma, one gets good or bad results according to his good or bad deeds performed in previous lives. This is why someone is born with talent—or with a silver spoon in his mouth—and somebody else takes birth with much less talent or in less favorable circumstances.

Of course, this is a very complicated subject matter, and it is difficult to know one's karma or destiny. Sometimes things can be set up so that you have a very good or very bad period in your life, and then, seemingly out of nowhere, things change completely. It is then just like Forrest Gump's mother saying: "Life is a box of chocolates, Forrest. You never know what you're gonna get."

If you are a tournament player, try your best; how can you do anything more? Accept that the result is never completely in your hands. This understanding, in and of itself, might not make you the next Tiger Woods in golf, but it will help you become a more peaceful and sane person. My technique and training aid, however, will certainly help you to become the best golfer you can be.

Appendices

In the appendices, you will find additional examples regarding the use of slow practice methods. These examples give additional weight to the ideas presented in this book and should help further strengthen your realization about the proper process of practice. Before presenting these quotations, I would like to express my deepest appreciation to the authors for their realizations. The methods and principles presented here are applicable for mastering any kind of physical skill.

Cognitive **Science**

Cognitive scientists say mastering a complex skill takes "ten years of deliberate practice." After a period of slow, conscious practice, however, skills are mastered. They then move into "the huge infrastructure of subconscious modules in which expertise you've already developed is stored" according to Dr. Bror Saxberg, chief learning officer at K12 Inc., a Herndon, Va., firm that develops online learning products. He says that there's "no short cut" to going through an initial period of slow practice in order to build any skill. The good news, according to Saxberg, is that mastering a skill doesn't depend on innate talent but "whether you have the will, patience and interest to put in that practice."

Another lesson from cognitive science is that minds do best "when they're challenged, but not too challenged." This is why there are golfers who are still not convinced about the benefits of slow motion practice. Because they are not able to maintain the correct internal attitude, they get bored by it. The benefit they derive is thus limited.

Dan Millman's **The Inner Athlete**

Dan Millman, a former world-champion athlete and college professor, considers slow motion practice a key to reaching the highest level of mastery. He says that it gives you time to be aware of every part of a movement, whether it's a baseball or golf swing, a javelin toss, or a karate punch. When you perform an activity in slow motion, you can sense such complex parts of the act as its weight shift and the coordination of body parts. Since most unconscious errors occur in the middle of a movement sequence, slowing the movement down can have surprising benefits. It can ease the speed of learning, because mistakes that were formerly hidden will become painfully obvious.

He presents an interesting test that he calls the Slow-Motion Experience:

> **Test 1**: Hold your right hand in front of your face, so that you are looking into your palm. Quickly move your right arm out to the side, turning your palm outward, and stop. Notice that you were aware of only the beginning and the end of that movement.

> **Test 2.** Now repeat the same sequence, but this time move your arm and hand in slow motion, slowly as you possibly can.

Let it take a full minute. Be aware of the relaxation of the arm and hand muscles. Notice how each finger turns; clearly see the different angles of your hand, as if for the first time.

"In this test, you were clearly aware of the movement of your arm and hand in its entirety, from beginning to end. I discovered, after a period of slow-motion practice, that I could move faster than ever because in moving slowly I became aware of tension and was able to let it go. Without tension, it's possible to move with blinding speed.

Slow-motion practice is like studying slow-motion instant-replay films of training, except that in practice you're also feeling, not just seeing. You can apply this technique to virtually every sport or movement form. It applies particularly well to activities like golf, baseball, tennis, and handball. In coaching gymnastics, I often carry athletes slowly through a somersaulting movement so that they can become aware of every part of turning over. Slowing down your practice expands your awareness and eliminates the blurred blind spot encountered in rapid movements. You can be very creative in applying slow motion to different activities. (If you figure out how to apply it to skydiving, of course, I'd like to hear about it.)

Slow motion works, and it's fun. Like the practitioners of T'ai Chi, you may even discover that slow-motion sport is a form of moving meditation." *The Inner Athlete*

Effortless Mastery by Kenny Werner

Kenny Werner is a world-class jazz pianist and teacher. In 1996, he published a book that has had a major impact on the music world: _Effortless Mastery_. Here is an excerpt from his book regarding the importance of deliberate, precise, and slow practice:

> "This practicing must be very focused, very intentional. The length of time you practice must be limited to the length of time you can remain in the space. Then you must STOP! or you will compromise the deliberateness of the practice. In this way, five or ten minutes of practice is preferable to two hours of rambling. I cannot overemphasize that, although your practicing seems unbearably slow, your playing really takes off! That kind of concentration and infinite patience makes the act of playing feel like a release. You feel as if you were riding a bicycle with the wind at your back. It may seem as if someone is playing for you while you're watching! Don't judge your progress by daily measure, but notice improvement in your playing over time. More maneuverability, more freedom, and more creativity will result."

Touretski **swimming** methods

Gennadi Touretski was the swimming coach of Alexander Popov, two-time Olympic gold medal winner and former holder of the world record for the one hundred meters freestyle. Daniel Drollette, a freelance science writer, commented on Touretski's swimming methods as follows:

> "The emphasis during training is on **quality of performance** rather than mileage. His idea is that with constant repetition, **precisely practised movements** become second nature-like reflexes. To work properly this training method demands **meticulous attention to detail**. 'If you can't do it exactly right, don't do it at all,' Touretski says. He'd rather have his swimmers do a few movements properly than do a lot of movements incorrectly. Touretski and his swimmers talk in terms of 'muscle memory.' ... So much time is spent on proper technique that by Olympic standards, Klim, Popov and the rest of Touretski's squad have relatively leisurely workouts - though they still swim about 70 kilometres a week.

> To outsiders, his methods appear odd. American coach, Bill Irwin, once told a reporter: 'Popov does long sets with meticulously precise strokes and a consistently beautiful flow. In three weeks,

I never saw him do a single lap that looked hard.' Part of what he saw is Touretski's super slow swimming method. Touretski demonstrates by walking across his office in exaggerated slow motion. By moving extremely slowly, he has to concentrate on the exact placement of each muscle. Balance becomes imperative. 'People are more wobbly when moving very slowly and they have to constantly shift weight to get their balance right,' he says. The same applies in the pool, and **when swimmers can travel smoothly at a very slow speed, they can move more smoothly at high speed.** Super slow swimming ... improves a swimmer's ability to relax at higher speed.

... Relaxation is often overlooked, but the great American swimmer Johnny Weissmuller once said that 'the greatest secret of freestyle swimming is relaxation at top speed.' ... Touretski elaborates: 'Not all muscles are switched on at the same time. There's a wave of muscles contracting or relaxing simultaneously.' Learning to relax the muscles that are not in use saves energy and staves off fatigue. Training at slow speed also helps the swimmer hone the all-important intuitive 'feel' of the water to anticipate, control and manipulate its flow. Swimmers get quite mystical when describing this ability, like artists describing 'a good eye' for painting."

The principle accepted by Touretski is universal: If you cannot practice right, don't practice at all. You can't practice right at full speed before you have completely mastered that skill having first done it slowly. However, even great masters in some disciplines practice slowly a great deal of time during their later practice sessions, in order to repair possible bad habits that might have crept in while performing their skill at full speed — or just to re-energize their batteries.

Martial Arts

Slow, smooth, accentuated, and precise movements are well known in the training of ancient martial arts. They are not practiced for the sake of their slowness, but as a means to an end: To discern and experience the motion in detail with body and mind.

> "Slow practice imprints your neural pathways with the same form that you will later use when moving at lightning speed. But at first you must make it slow to make sure it's right. As your practice continues, the neural paths become stronger. But you're not ready for fast moves yet.
>
> As your practice strengthens certain axon/dendrite patterns, you will notice that performing the movement requires less conscious supervision with respect to how you hold your arms or legs, the path that they travel, etc. The technique seems to flow, and your execution acquires a smooth quality. Now you are ready to increase your speed.
>
> Don't try for blurring speed all at once, though. When you first notice how smooth and effortless your technique has become, you'll be tempted to pour on the speed. Okay, go ahead and try a few reps, but then go back to your slo-mo speed and

gradually increase the pace. Otherwise, jumping to warp speed may result in allowing sloppiness to creep in.

You can use this learning method in both empty hand and weapons practice. If you follow this model, your movements will be clean, crisp and faster than a speeding bullet. And others will think that you have access to some secret, advanced techniques, when all you've done is master the basics." — WARSKYL: *A Page For Christian Martialists*

Daniel **Bonade's** teachings

Daniel Bonade, a master of the clarinet, was speaking on principles of psycho-motor learning that scientists have only recently begun to understand. Experienced performers in every discipline have known for centuries that the way to acquire physical skill is through slow practice. He wrote in the 1950's:

> "The method of acquiring technique is to train your fingers to do very slowly what they will be called upon to do rapidly. Practice the passage slowly, repeating it many times in order to form the correct path in the mind – like drawing a pattern in wet cement, which, when set, will endure. After sufficient slow practice, perfectly even practice, speed is easy to achieve. The fingers will know where to go even at a pace too fast for the eye."

Mind, Muscle, and Music by Frank R. Wilson, M.D.

Dr. Wilson is assistant clinical professor of neurology at the University of California School of Medicine, San Francisco. As a neurologist, he became interested in the process involved in the acquisition of musical skill. However, his findings apply to mastering any physical skill, as well. Neurologist Frank R. Wilson states:

> "Slow practice is the key to rapid technical progress. The cerebellum is a non-judgmental part of the brain: it assumes that any repetitive activity in the muscular system is being repeated because the conscious mind is trying to make it automatic. The cerebellum will be just as efficient an automatizer of incorrect sequences of timing as of those that are correct. When practicing takes place at a pace too fast for accurate playing, there is very little chance for the material to be mastered, and reliable, confident performance simply will not occur."

Special note

In September, 2010, Rick Malm (SSC Golf Swing) contacted me with the desire to test the training method presented in the book you just read. He was impressed with the concepts, and he proposed that I guide him through the training process. He said that he would then give me all the data acquired for my future use. He is an expert with a lot of experience in sports and has a scientific background. As such, this was a good opportunity to thoroughly test the method.

The whole process is documented in a video ebook (videos embedded in PDF document) that can be previewed and/or purchased on thesolarsweetspot.com website. It should be a great help for anybody trying to follow the practice principles of this book.

After a period of testing process, Rick Malm wrote the following summary and overall impression of the process: "It takes a lot of discipline. Most of the people I know would not take the time. The progress takes months and 1000's of swings. Unlike many training processes, the sweet spot training requires constant testing of exact sweet spot error distances and a self awareness training process that teaches the body/mind how to work more effectively. This is a long road to travel. Even after 6 months I feel like I still have a long way to go to master the subject. It's difficult to stay motivated on your own without a coach helping you every day with analysis and motivation.

Why was I attracted to this training method? Nobody understands how to teach this subject and it can make a difference of a win or loss at long drive world championship for my clients, and for me it means the difference of hitting fairways and greens as well as losing golf balls in the rough. I wish I would have learned this teaching technique before I started playing golf and other sports."

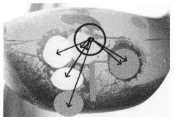

Picture 11. Comparison of Rick's full-speed swing sweet spot accuracy in a time span of three months.

References

I acknowledge and thank the copyright-holders (authors and publishers) of every work I quote from in this book.

Hogan, Ben. (1985). *Five Lessons: The Modern Fundamentals of Golf*. First Fireside Edition.

Hogan, Ben. (1985). *Power Golf*. First Fireside Edition.

Andreas, Jamey. (1999). *The Principles of Correct Practice for Guitar*. Seven Eyes Publications.

Chang, Chuan C. (2004). *Fundamentals of Piano Practice*. 2nd Edition.

Clampett, Bobby. (2007). *The Impact Zone: Mastering Golf's Moment of Truth*. Thomas Dunne Books.

Darling, John. (n.d.). *Power Golf Academy*. Retrieved Februar 2008, from Square Impact: www.powergolfinstruction.com/id77.html

Drollette, Daniel. (1998). Swimming Technique: Swim Like a Fish. *New Scientist , No2145*.

Gallwey, Timothy. (1986). *The Inner Game of Golf*. Pan Macmillan.

Gravelbelly. (2008, June 21). *WARSKYL: A Page For Christian Martialists*. Retrieved Dezember 16, 2008, from Adwanced Techniques:

http://warskyl.blogspot.com/2008/06/advanced-techniques.html

Larsen, Grey. (2004). *The Essential Tin Whistle Toolbox.* Mel Bay Publications.

Millman, Dan. (1994). *The Inner Athlete.* Stillpoint Publishing.

Ortega, Lana. (n.d.). *Golf Tips Magazine* . Retrieved June 10, 2008, from Myth busters: www.golftipsmag.com/instruction/strategy/troubleshooting/myth-busters_4.html

Prabhupada, A.C. Bhaktivedanta Swami. (2007). *Bhagavad-gita As It Is.* Krishna Books Inc.

How the Bhagavad Gita landed on a golf course. Retrieved March 2008, from http://www.hinduismtoday.com/archives/2001/3-4/16_bagger_vance.shtml, *Hinduism today,* March/April 2001 (Rosen, Steven J.)

Wilson, Frank R. (1981). *Mind, Muscle and Music: Physiological Clues to Better Teaching.* CA Selmer.

Made in the USA
Monee, IL
18 April 2022